This book belongs to:

THE KARASICK CHILD SAFETY INITIATIVE of PROJECT Y.E.S.

Let's Stay Safe!

The Malka and Arthur Krausman Edition

Illustrated by Tova Leff

Published by
Mesorah Publications, ltd

in conjunction with **PROJECT Y.E.S.**

Introduction

How can we ensure the safety of our children? This question is at the top of every parent's list of priorities, and in the complex and ever-changing world in which we live, it is more important than ever that we train our children properly so they can remain safe and secure.

This picture book was designed to provide parents with a comfortable and *tzanua* (modest) way to speak to children about a broad range of safety matters, including the need to protect their personal space and privacy.

As with so many other areas in life, moderation is the key as far as parental anxiety is concerned when having safety talks with your kids. A total absence of anxiety on your part will not convey the importance of these messages, but if you are too tense, your child becomes unnerved and focuses more on your apprehension than what you are discussing with him/her.

In order to assist you in achieving the global goal of raising well-adjusted children, important reading material and a link to a video presentation are available on the Project YES website, www.kosherjewishparenting.com, in the Child Safety Initiative section. We urge you, if possible, to review these materials, preferably before you read this book to your children.

An extraordinary amount of reflection and thought went into the language and illustrations of this book and we would like to express our appreciation to Mrs. Bracha Goetz, who wrote the original text of these pages and remained available whenever needed, and to Mrs. Tova Leff for her illustrations which are fun-filled, yet rich in content.

We are grateful to Drs. David Pelcovitz and Benzion Twerski who graciously gave of their time to plan, edit, and review the text and illustrations in order to present the messages effectively.

We deeply appreciate the generosity of Project YES Vice Chairman, Mark Karasick, and his wife, Linda, for dedicating our Child Safety Initiative, in memory of both their mothers who recently passed away, and that of my childhood friends Moish and Esther Konig, for dedicating this volume in memory of her parents.

Rabbis Meir Zlotowitz and Nosson Scherman were personally involved with this project. We thank them sincerely, as we do Reb Gedaliah Zlotowitz and Reb Avrohom Biderman for shepherding the book to completion.

Mrs. Chaya Becker, administrative director of The Center for Jewish Family Life/Project YES, was the driving force behind this book. Its readers owe her their gratitude.

To our dear children: Baruch & Alanna, Shlomie & Kaila, Leah & Moshe, Faigy & Dovid Meir, and, of course Sara; thank you for sharing me so graciously with our community and for giving Mommy and me such unending nachas over the past thirty years. I look forward to reading this book to our grandchildren, Dovi, Miri, Leah, Arielle, and Gila.

My wife Udi offered her incredible range of talents and served as the production manager of this project. She is an amazing mother to our children, and always ready to fill any void when my duties take me away from home. May Hashem repay her with our greatest wish — that we grow old together in good health, and share nachas from our wonderful children and grandchildren.

Finally, and most importantly, I humbly give thanks to Hashem for allowing me to have a part in keeping His children safe and secure so that they can grow into proud, well-adjusted, and accomplished adults.

Yakov Horowitz
Director, Center for Jewish Family Life / Project Y.E.S.

19 Tammuz 5771, Monsey NY

רבות בנות עשו חיל ואת עלית על כולנה

לז״נ **מרת פסיה ב״ר יצחק ע״ה**

ולז״נ **מרת ראצי ב״ר זאב ע״ה**

We are proud to dedicate the Project YES Child Safety Initiative
In memory of our dear mothers

Pepa Karasick ע״ה and **Ruth Ulevitch Lang** ע״ה

Our mothers were great women who made an impact on their respective Jewish communities. They are both remembered as refined individuals who, in their own gentle way, let their feelings be known and their presence felt. We feel privileged to continue their legacy.

May the merit of all lives that are improved as a result of this safety initiative be a *zechus* for their *neshamos*.

תהא זכרן ברוך

Mark and Linda Karasick

Zev and Shoshana Karasick, Adina, Hillel and Perela

Yakov Karasick

Avi Karasick

Yitzi and Terri Karasick, Ali, Rafi and Pacey

טוב שם משמן טוב

לז״נ **אהרן צבי ב״ר יהושע ז״ל**

וזוגתו **מלכה ב״ר משה יצחק ע״ה**

The Project YES *Let's Stay Safe* picture book is dedicated in memory of our beloved parents

Malka and Arthur Krausman, ע״ה

Never seeking honor or accolades, they supported and welcomed needy and forlorn members of our society into their home. Bikur Cholim was their trademark, tirelessly visiting hospital patients and cheering up shut-ins in their apartments as well. Their warm and friendly smiles were well-known in Belle Harbor, on Ocean Parkway, and in Miami Beach. Their love for their own children and grandchildren and all Jewish children was legendary, and it is our hope that this picture book dedicated in their memory will improve the lives of Jewish children worldwide; helping them lead safe, secure, and meaningful lives.

May their memories be blessed forever.

Esther and Moish Konig

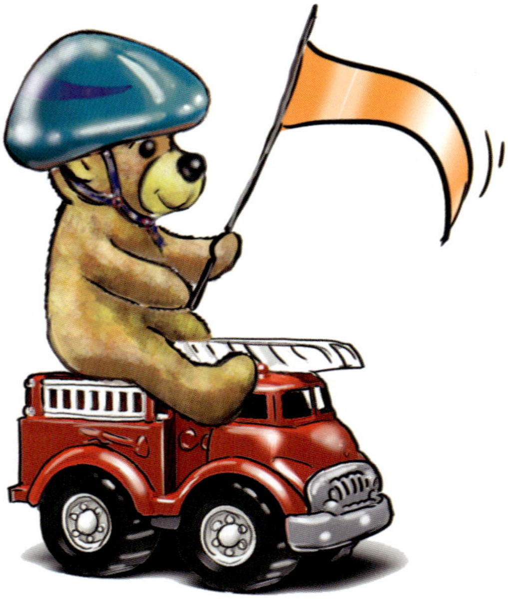

Hashem wants us to stay safe.
But we've got to know how.
It's a mitzvah in the Torah.
Let's start right now!

Want to hear what I know?
See if you know it too.
Here are some safety rules
we're smart enough to do.

I'm getting bigger,
and so, you see,
I can ride my two-wheeler
really fast — look at me!

I always wear a helmet,
'cause if I go thump,
on top of my head
who needs a big bump?

Crossing the street
must be done carefully.
We cross at the corner,
to make sure we can see.

And let's say my ball
bounces way out there,
I won't go to get it!
No way! I don't dare!

If a driver ever stops us
asking which way to go,
we stay far away,
unless it's someone we know.

But if it's a stranger
we run away so fast,
until we're absolutely sure
that the car has passed!

Playing is fun together with friends.
Can you go to their house? It really depends.
Just ask Mommy first, before you go to play.
She always has to know where you're spending your day.

If someone comes knocking,
I don't open the door,
unless I have permission.
I need to be sure!

I've got my own knapsack,
my drawer, my private space,
and I keep lots of stuff
in my own special place.

My body's also private.
It's not for all to see.
Some of it stays covered.
That's just how it should be.

Being with big kids and grownups
is always loads of fun.
I've learned to fly a kite,
and even hit a home run!

But even someone we know
and like very much
shouldn't touch us in ways
we don't want them to touch.

And if I'm not sure
if a touch was right or wrong,
I'd ask my Daddy or Mommy —
and not wait too long!

Even if someone touched me
a very long time ago,
I'll surely tell them;
it's best that they know.

17

I'd tell Mommy or Daddy
if someone I meet
tells me to keep a secret
and then offers a treat.

If someone says, "Let's go someplace alone,
only you and me."
"No way!" I'd reply.
That's not a safe place to be!

We can always say, "No!"
and quickly go away.
When we don't feel comfortable,
we don't have to stay!

If someone tells me a secret
that to my parents I should not say,
I always trust my parents,
I'd tell them that very day!

Medicine and vitamins
stay high up on a shelf.
Taking things like that,
I would never do myself.

I make sure that the baby
doesn't get a small toy
she can put in her mouth;
I'm quite a careful boy!

I know that matches
are not safe for me.
Hot pots and candles —
I just let them be!

And you know those knobs
on the stove used for cooking?
I don't play with them ever,
even when no one's looking!

If clothes catch on fire,
how fast can you be?
Stop, Drop, and Roll.
Let's practice, you and me!

We have a fire plan for our family,
to get out of our house as quick as can be.
There's a special place where we'll run and stay,
so the firemen will know we're out and okay.

Once I got lost,
but not anymore!
I stay with my Mommy,
on the street or in a store.
If you ever get lost,
do you know what to do?
You call out real loudly,
so Mommy can find you!

But let's say you're yelling and she still doesn't hear?
Then you should go and find a cashier.
    If you don't see one, don't wander — just try
to ask a mommy, who's walking nearby.

Or find a policeman; he will help you.
But staying near Mommy, is the best thing to do!

It's really good to know your address!
And your phone number too, so you won't have to guess.

28

If I see something dangerous,
I'll call 9-1-1.
If we ever smell gas,
outside we should run!

Look, we're getting bigger.
Hashem helped us grow!
And there is already
so much that we know!

We want to stay safe;
we've learned lots we can do.
We'll remember these rules.
We hope you do too!

To follow these rules,
we'll all do our best.
And we'll daven to Hashem,
He'll do the rest.

Always Remember These Safety Rules:

- Always wear a helmet when you ride a bicycle or scooter.
- Cross streets carefully at the corner, and don't run into the street.
- Stay away from a car if you don't know the driver, even to give directions.
- Get permission from a parent before going somewhere to play.
- Never let strangers into the house without permission.
- Your body belongs to you, just like your private space at home.
- Only your parents or a doctor can touch you in a private space that is covered by a bathing suit.
- Don't let grown-ups do things to you that make you feel uncomfortable. If they do, just say "no" and walk away.
- If someone made you feel uncomfortable, tell your parents, even if it happened long ago.
- Ask your mother or father if you are not sure whether the way someone touched you is okay or not.
- Don't go with someone to a place where you'll be the only two people.
- If someone tells you to not to tell your parents what he is doing to you, tell them right away — they will be happy you told them.
- All medicine must stay on a high shelf or safe place, and small toys must be kept away from little children.
- Never touch matches, hot pots, candles, or knobs on the stove.
- If there is fire on your body or clothing; "stop, drop, and roll".
- Ask your parents if they have a fire safety plan, and where you should meet in case you all have to leave the house because of an emergency.
- Always stay near your mother or father. If you get lost, call for them. If you can't find them, go to a cashier, a mother, or a policeman.
- Learn your address, phone number, 911, and the number of Hatzalah.
- If you smell gas, tell everyone and run outside immediately.
- Of course, always *daven* to Hashem to keep you safe.